Communicate Your Feelings
(without starting a fight)

Personal Workbook

Table of Contents

Table of Contents, cont.

Gift

Communication Techniques List

Get it at **www.nicsaluppo.com/gifts**.

If you didn't get it yet, there's a Communication Techniques List waiting for you at the above link. The list serves as a refresher when you're in a pinch and don't have time to refer back to the book or workbook.

The Communication Techniques List is a downloadable PDF you can save on your computer, phone, hang on your refrigerator, tape to your steering wheel, or keep at your desk. It's an easily scannable list you can quickly refer to at any moment. Use it as a tool when you need a quick reminder.

Welcome

Welcome to your personal workbook, where you'll ingrain the communication techniques found in the book. Here, you'll do exercises to help you make the 13 communication techniques more and more natural for you.

This workbook doesn't operate as a standalone, so if you haven't read the book, it probably won't make much sense to you. It's meant to ingrain what's in the book, not replace it. The book explains the *why* and *how* of each communication technique. This workbook assumes you've already read about the why and how and are in a personal space of wanting to practice and make the techniques into habits. With that in mind, if you haven't read the book, do that before completing this workbook.

~

You're about to get started, but before you do, make sure you have a copy of the book handy. You'll need it to follow along and find answers. The answers to all questions requiring a specific answer, such as Fill in the Blank and Multiple Choice questions, are organized at the back of this workbook starting on **page 90**. While nobody's stopping you from just flipping to the answers in the back, you're not encouraged to do that. If you're completing this workbook for personal development reasons, you're highly encouraged to refer back to the original book to find answers. After all, you're here because you want to be, not because you're being forced to do this. So, don't just find the answer in the back and move on as if it's a homework assignment.

Once you've found the answers in the original book, *then* check the answer key in the back to confirm your answer. If you got stuck and couldn't find the answer or didn't understand a certain answer, go ahead and set this workbook down and reread that section of the book to make the concept stick in your mind. This way, when the time comes to utilize a concept in real time during an interaction with your partner, you'll be able to draw upon it. Speaking of that, I hope you and your partner will give each other some leeway.

Understand that you're learning these concepts, and may not be able to automatically draw upon them during an interaction just yet. Of course, the goal is to be able to draw on them at any moment, and the assumption is that you're making the effort to learn them. But talk with your partner in advance and agree that you'll give one another the time and space to refer back to this workbook or the Communication Techniques List. Don't laugh at one another for trying to use a tool that'll improve your communication. For both of you, commit to making your best effort at completing this workbook while also giving the leeway to take your conversations slowly so there's space to refer to what you've been learning here.

Alternatively, you might be the only one in a partnership who has read the book and is completing this workbook, and that's okay, too. Commit to making your best effort at ingraining the concepts and to giving yourself time and space during conversations to consider how you'd like to respond. Do you remember the simple diagram of two overlapping circles in the original book at the end of Communication Technique #8? By working on yourself, the entire relationship can't help but improve.

Introduction

Please note that this is a personal workbook. That means it's about you, the person completing it. It's about you reflecting on yourself and becoming a more effective communicator. That's probably a given for those of you completing this workbook, but my concern is that some people will complete it with the intention of working on their partner, not on themselves. So, if you're completing this to work on your partner, and not to deeply reflect upon yourself, you'll be quite frustrated since it wasn't designed for that purpose.

Additionally, this workbook was designed for people who are really interested in self-examination. Not just interested, but *really* interested. Many of the questions will require something of you. Namely, they'll require a commitment to the truth of what psychological and emotional dynamics are taking place within you. This isn't only about changing how you speak and behave externally; it's about undergoing an internal transformation that pours over into your external interactions.

Some of the exercises do have correct and incorrect answers, but many of the reflection questions are open-ended. What this means is that you'll have to read the question and then bring your awareness inside yourself to find the answer. In these cases, the only correct answer is the truth of what's taking place inside you emotionally and psychologically. This isn't about what you *should* think, feel, or believe; it's about what you *do* think, feel, and believe. It might require a new level of self-honesty to acknowledge your true answers to the self-reflection questions, so the courage to see yourself as you are and not as you wish to be is required.

Self-reflection can sometimes be painful, especially when what you find doesn't align with who you've worked so hard to convince the world you are. But that's what it takes to transform how you do relationships. In fact, it's what it takes to actually be in a relationship. In other words, it takes seeing and knowing yourself deeply so that you can accept being seen and known deeply by someone else. Again, you must see and know yourself deeply to be capable of accepting someone else seeing and knowing you deeply.

If this sounds like a little more than you were bargaining for, I'd again like to say **Welcome!** While deep self-examination can be intimidating, it's also the only way out of old patterns. Remember, refusing to see ourselves as we are prevents us from becoming who we wish to be. Seeing ourselves as we are opens the gateway to becoming who we wish to be.

~

The questions in this workbook are meant to expand your self-awareness. Therefore, if you read a question and your immediate answer is, "I don't know," that's okay, but don't skip the question. It just means you'll have to take some time to become aware of the answer.

To explore a question you don't have an immediate answer to, use this three step process:

1. Pause

2. Reflect

3. Write

As an example, if you read a question and immediately think, *I don't know*, instead of skipping ahead, **pause**. It's okay that you don't know. My therapist asks me questions all the time that I don't have an immediate answer to, and I like that. I like it because it gives me the opportunity to become self-aware of something I wasn't previously aware of. If I immediately knew the answers to everything he asked, I wouldn't be gaining insight, I'd just be rattling off what I already know. When I don't immediately know an answer to a question he asks, I pause and bring my awareness inward. I'm not using my analytical brain to figure it out; I'm pausing (i.e., remaining still) and noticing what answers naturally arise from within myself.

Reflecting isn't an exercise in problem solving. It's noticing what arises within you. For example, if you were asked, "Why do I avoid hard conversations with my partner?" and your immediate answer is, "I don't know. I'm just not confrontational," rather than immediately move on, you can pause. Get still and bring your attention inward. Have your mind's awareness on your feet, legs, gut, and heart. Be aware of those areas and notice what responses arise. Gently ask yourself, "Why do I avoid hard conversations with my partner?" then, notice the answers that come up naturally and spontaneously. Don't think your way to an answer, notice the answer arise from within.

Next, **reflect** the answer back to yourself by repeating it. If the answer, "Because I'm terrified of abandonment but don't want to admit it," comes up, repeat it gently in your mind.

Finally, **write**. Write your answer down. DO NOT analyze whether it "should" be the answer. Just put down whatever comes up for you. From there you can say, "Okay, that's a start, but I think there's more," or, "Okay, that's a start, but something doesn't seem quite complete about that answer." Pause again, bring your awareness back inside yourself, and see what additional responses arise from within. Continue this process until you have a sense of your answer being complete.

Your answer is complete when you have an authentic sense of fulfillment, satisfaction, or peace about your responses. That doesn't mean more insight relating to the question won't come up later. But for now, this moment, is it complete? Or, is there an internal, nagging sense that there's more self-awareness or insight to explore right here and now? If it's complete for now, good, go ahead and move on. Just don't move on from a question merely because it's difficult. Give yourself the time and space to ask the questions and then see what kinds of responses you discover from within.

If you're newer to self-reflection, bookmark this page so you can refer back to the explanation of this process as often as needed until it becomes natural for you.

~

In getting started, let's go through a quick refresher of the 13 communication techniques.

Communicate Your Feelings (without starting a fight) contains four sections:

I.   Avoiding Language that Provokes Escalation

II.   Clarifying Your Thoughts and Feelings

III.   When You've Made a Mistake

IV.   Responding to Your Partner's Feelings

Within each section are the following 13 communication techniques:

Section I: Avoiding Language that Provokes Escalation

Communication Technique #1: "When"
Instead of saying "Always . . ." or "Never . . ." say, "When . . ."

Communication Technique #2: "I Would Like"
Instead of saying, "Should . . ." or "Shouldn't . . ." say, "I would like . . ."

Communication Technique #3: "I Feel Angry"
Instead of name-calling or insulting, say, "I feel angry."

Communication Technique #4: "This is Challenging for Me"
Instead of saying nothing, say, "This is challenging for me."

Section II: Clarifying Your Thoughts and Feelings

Communication Technique #5: "I Think and I Feel"
Instead of saying, "I feel like . . ." say, "I think X and I feel Y about that."

Communication Technique #6: "I Feel"
Instead of saying, "You make me feel," say, "I feel . . ."

Section III: When You've Made a Mistake

Communication Technique #7: "I Was Wrong"
Instead of saying, "Look what you made me do," say, "I was wrong."

Communication Technique #8: "~~I Apologize~~" "I'm Sorry"
Instead of saying, "I apologize," say, "I'm sorry."

Section IV: Responding to Your Partner's Feelings

Communication Technique #9: "It's Great You're Letting This Out"
Instead of saying, "Don't cry," say, "It's great you're letting this out."

Communication Technique #10: Let Them Be Upset with You
Instead of saying, "Don't be upset with me," say, "You can be upset with me as long as you want."

Communication Technique #11: Set a Boundary
Instead of meeting disrespect with more disrespect, set a boundary.

Communication Technique #12: "I'm Happy You Want to Improve"
Instead of viewing it as a personal attack, view it as a good thing they want to improve the relationship.

Communication Technique #13: Examine Both Sides
Instead of blaming, examine both sides of the situation.

Let's jump in and begin ingraining the techniques.

*Need Extra Writing Space?

While I've erred on the side of ensuring you have plenty of writing space for each question, there's also extra writing space in the back of this workbook starting on **page 80**. If you run out of writing space for a particular question but have more examples, instances, situations, thoughts, feelings, or insights you want to write down, you are absolutely encouraged to do so by flipping to the back and using the extra space.

PART I
Avoiding Language that Provokes Escalation

Everyone wants to be heard. How do you respond when you're in a space of wanting to be heard but fear you won't be heard or sense your partner isn't hearing you? Examples of common responses are explosive or aggressive communication, sarcasm, put-downs, name-calling, withdrawing, staying silent, and being purposefully nonresponsive.

Below, write down all the ways you respond when you want to be heard but fear the other person won't or can't hear you:

_____

_____

_____

_____

_____

_____

_____

_____

_____

Communication Technique #1
"When"
Instead of saying "Always . . ." or "Never . . ." say, "When . . ."

*A*lways and *never* are absolute terms that breed defensiveness and argumentation. When you're tempted to tell your partner "You always . . ." or "You never . . ." what's the feeling you're experiencing in that moment?

Think back to a time when you used an absolute term on your partner such as *always* or *never*. For example, "You never help me clean," or "You always avoid cleaning." Write down the sentence you said to your partner at that time:

_____

_____

_____

_____

In the instance you wrote down above, what feeling were you experiencing in your body at the time? As examples, people might experience anger, frustration, fear, or sadness when they're using absolute terms like *always* or *never*.

_____

_____

_____

_____

Use what you wrote down on the previous page and rephrase it using the word *When* and then add the feeling you wrote down. For example, "You never help me clean" becomes, "When you don't help me clean for months at a time, I feel upset and hurt." As another example, "You never act like you care about me" becomes "When you act in these certain ways (list them), I experience that as you not caring about me and I feel hurt and upset about that."

The key in this communication technique is that you're sticking with *your* experience: *When X happens, here's how I experience it and this is the emotion I feel in my body related to X happening.*

Write down your specific example using *When* plus the feeling you experienced related to the situation.

_____

_____

_____

_____

_____

_____

_____

_____

_____

_____

Now, make your Big Ask using the phrase *Would you be willing?* Remember, tone is vital here, so when you make your Big Ask, be sincere, genuine, and kind. Many people make a Big Ask that's perfectly reasonable, but the tone they use causes them to come across as a Big Ass.

Write down your rephrased sentence from above. Using the same example, this would be, "When you don't help me clean for months at a time, I feel upset and hurt." Next, add your Big Ask as its own separate sentence. For example, "Would you be willing to wipe the countertops and unload the dishwasher three days out of the week?"

_____

_____

_____

_____

_____

_____

_____

_____

_____

_____

_____

Communication Technique #2
"I Would Like"

Instead of saying, "Should . . ." or "Shouldn't . . ." say, "I would like . . ."

Stop using the S-word twins on yourself and your partner! The underlying message of the word "should" is that there's something wrong with you if you *don't do* that thing. Likewise, the underlying message of the word "shouldn't" is that there's something wrong with you if you *do* that thing. "Should" and "shouldn't" are nasty words that will likely be received with defensiveness, not openness. So, how can you rephrase something when you're tempted to use the S-words?

Below, you should rephrase the sentences using "I would like . . ." instead of "should." Also, did you catch what happened in that previous sentence? If you did, great, you've been practicing the concepts in the book. If you didn't catch it, well, you should really pay more attention. Did you catch that one? If you didn't catch either of them, it's time to reread this section of the book!

Rephrase the below sentences using "I would like . . ." phrases. First, state "I would like," then state what you would like, then finish with a reason why you would like it that way.

You shouldn't fold the laundry like that. You should fold it like this. _____

_____

_____

You shouldn't leave the dishes in the sink. You should wash them right away. _____

_____

_____

You should do more to help around the house. _____

_____

_____

Since those examples were all in the book, here are a few fresh ones.

Rephrase the below sentences using "I would like . . ."

You shouldn't wait until your tank is on E to fill it up. _____

_____

_____

You should workout more often. _____

_____

_____

You should get help. _____

_____

_____

You shouldn't use the word "should." _____

_____

_____

You should forgive that person. _____

_____

_____

Communication Technique #3
"I Feel Angry"
Instead of name-calling or insulting, say, "I feel angry."

Feeling angry and frustrated from time to time is normal. The issue isn't feeling angry, the issue is how that anger is expressed. If expressed effectively, it can deepen and strengthen your relationship. If expressed through name-calling and insults, it will create a chasm between the two of you. Additionally, if you shove your anger down in the name of keeping the peace, this too will create a gap between you and your partner.

Are you likely to express your anger through name-calling, yelling, and insults? Or are you more likely to handle your anger through avoidant behaviors such as pushing it down into your body, keeping quiet, and withdrawing from the other person? Write down the unhealthy ways you handle your anger. Reflect back on at least three specific instances when you were angry at your partner and how you handled those instances.

_____

_____

_____

_____

_____

_____

_____

Self-reflect on how it is for you to directly state, "I feel angry" to your partner.

If you tend more toward lashing out and spewing insults, reflect on how it is to stick with what you're feeling instead of tearing down the other person. Why is it so important to tear them down? If you tend more toward shoving your anger down into your body and disengaging, reflect on how it is to actually say "I feel angry" out loud to your partner. Why is it so important to keep your feelings of anger hidden from them?

_____

_____

_____

_____

_____

_____

_____

_____

_____

_____

_____

_____

When you're angry, it can be hard to acknowledge your partner's viewpoint. But it's their viewpoint. No-body's saying you have to agree with it and nobody's saying that you don't get to share your perspective. But immediately shooting down your partner's viewpoint accomplishes only one thing: Your partner having a lack of emotional safety around you.

When your partner has a viewpoint you don't agree with, how do you normally respond?

_____

_____

_____

_____

_____

_____

_____

_____

_____

_____

_____

Write down at least one instance when you felt upset, hurt, or angry but then later found out you misread the situation. In such situations, your feelings were real, but your reasons for feeling that way weren't thoroughly evaluated. As an example, I once got into the car and caught my wife scrolling through my Facebook app on my phone. I was not happy. I was angry. Then I looked closer and saw the phone in her hand had a case with rounded corners. Mine has shock-absorbing flat corners. It was her phone she was on, not mine. I can self-validate that my anger was real in that moment, but my reasons for it were not well-explored. Don't skip this exercise—it's important you see that you've had at least one moment when your feelings were real but your reasons for those feelings were not thoroughly investigated. By seeing this in yourself, you'll be able to hold space for it in your partner. If you can't or won't see this in yourself, then you'll be severely impatient when you think your partner's reasons for being upset aren't based on hard facts.

_____

_____

_____

_____

_____

_____

_____

_____

_____

_____

Fill in the Blank

____ ____ ____ ____ ____ ____ ____ ____ are never invalid,

but the ____ ____ ____ ____ ____ ____ ____

for the ____ ____ ____ ____ ____ ____ ____ ____ can be discussed, examined, and evaluated.

Multiple Choice: Choose the best answer

If I'm angry or overwhelmed in a discussion and I take a break from the discussion to process my feelings, who's responsibility is it to reengage with the conversation?

    A. My partner's

    B. My child's, who plays a peacekeeper/fixer/mediator role

    C. Anyone but me

    D. Oh God, please, not me

    E. Mine

What is your responsibility?

    A. How another adult behaves

    B. The harmful words of another adult

    C. Your feelings pertaining to any given situation

Communication Technique #4
"This is Challenging for Me"
Instead of saying nothing, say, "This is challenging for me."

This one's for the avoiders! Calling all disengagers, disconnectors, withdrawers. To the people who have a million thoughts, feelings, and opinions swirling around on the inside but never engage your vocal cords and move your mouth to tell your partner what they are, I see you!

Growing up, did you ever attempt to express your feelings? If not, why not? If you did express your feelings, how were they received and responded to by your parents or caregivers?

_____

_____

_____

_____

_____

_____

_____

_____

What are three beliefs you currently hold about expressing your feelings today as an adult?

_____

_____

_____

_____

_____

_____

_____

_____

_____

_____

_____

_____

How has not discussing or not expressing your feelings affected your relationship?

_____

_____

_____

_____

_____

_____

_____

_____

_____

_____

Do you wait for your partner to draw your feelings out? Evaluate and write about how your experiences during childhood have driven you to wait for someone to draw out your feelings. Next, write down three self-encouraging, self-inspiring statements you can say to yourself to begin proactively sharing your feelings with your partner without relying on them to draw it out of you. Come back to these when you notice yourself stuck, disengaging, or withdrawing.

_____

_____

_____

_____

_____

_____

_____

_____

_____

_____

_____

_____

Fill in the Blank

I'm not actually waiting for the right time to communicate. I'm waiting for the _____ _____ _____ _____

and _____ _____ _____ _____ _____ _____ _____about

_____ _____ _____ _____ _____ _____ _____ _____ _____ _____ _____ _____ _____ to go away.

Emotional overwhelm is a very real issue. In difficult conversations, someone experiencing emotional overwhelm becomes flooded with intense feelings. Since the feelings are so intense, they don't know what to do with them, so they withdraw and shut down.

This is a tricky situation because on one hand, it's a response that gets its origin from a past trauma or series of past emotional wounds that started during your developmental years. But on the other hand, not taking responsibility for working through this issue means you can't engage in your relationship, which not only harms you but also your partner.

The good news is that awareness is half the process. *Without* awareness, you'll identify with the over-whelming feelings and shut down. *With* awareness, you can observe the overwhelming feelings and handle them in a way that allows you to avoid shutting down. Below are several ways to respond to emotional overwhelm and prevent withdrawal. All of them revolve around body movement. Movement is vital because the key is to move the emotions, not shove them back down where they came from.

Read over the list below and then commit to the plan you'll write out in the next step.

When I notice I'm becoming overwhelmed and at risk of shutting down, I'll take a break from the conversation, go to a private space, and:

- Hop up and down while shaking my arms
- Hit a pillow with my fists
- Punch the air
- Lie on my back and kick my legs
- Lie on my back on the bed and pound my fists and kick my legs
- Run in place
- Move my hands and arms through the air in a flowing motion, much like a combination of dancing and tai chi
- Hit a bed, chair, couch, or pillow with half of a swim noodle
- Do jumping jacks
- Stand with wide feet, put my hands on my hips, and breathe with an open chest and tall posture
- Stand with wide feet and raise my arms over my head, back down, and repeat many times
- Put on music and dance

One of the first things people ask is if they can do pushups, workout, or go for a run. No, no, and no. Notice that none of the movements suggested are difficult, requiring strong muscle contractions. A hard workout is going to take your mind off your emotions, the exact opposite of what you want.

The key to making this process work is moving your body while simultaneously feeling your emotions. Once you get down and start doing pushups, your mind is on the difficulty of the muscle contraction. I don't care who you are, even if you're Dwayne Johnson, doing a pushup is harder than punching the air. This isn't about exhausting your energy. What it is about is moving your body—the opposite of shutting down—so your overwhelming emotions can finally move out of you instead of going back down into the basement of your psyche. Intense emotions might come to the surface while you're doing this movement. Good. It's an opportunity for them to be expressed out of your body instead of depressed back inside. Shout, cry, yell, sob. Do it into a pillow if you must, but above all else, don't shove it back down into yourself.

The next time I notice overwhelming feelings coming up in a conversation with my partner, instead of identifying with them and shutting down, I will observe the feelings and:

_____

_____

_____

_____

_____

_____

_____

_____

PART II
Clarifying Your Thoughts and Feelings

Fill in the Blank

A feeling isn't a _____ _____ _____ _____ _____ _____ _____

and a _____ _____ _____ _____ _____ _____ _____ isn't a feeling.

Communication Technique #5
"I Think and I Feel"

Instead of saying, "I feel like . . ." say, "I think X and I feel Y about that."

One example of the Thought-Feeling Mishmash is "I feel like you don't care about me." Below, give another example of the Thought-Feeling Mishmash:

_____

_____

_____

_____

Multiple Choice: Choose the best answer

Which of these statements accurately separates thoughts from feelings?

    A. I feel it would be best to not go to this event.

    B. I feel like it wouldn't be a good idea to go to this event.

    C. I'm not feeling like going to this event.

    D. None of the above.

Fill in the Blank

A **thought** is something you experience in your head in the form of

_____ _____ _____ _____ _____ and _____ _____ _____ _____ _____ _____.

A **feeling** is something you experience in your _____ _____ _____ _____ in the form of

physiological _____ _____ _____ _____ _____ _____ _____ _____ _____ _____.

Which of the following are feelings? Which are descriptive words of feelings? Which are neither? Put a checkmark next to the feelings (✓), a dot next to the descriptive words of feelings (•), and an X (**x**) next to those that are neither.

Fear	Rejected	Terror
Therapy	Paranoid	Less than
Sky	Abandoned	Anger
Empty	Ugly	Confident
Rage	Mountains	Powerful
Humiliated	Unreliable	Anxiety
Impulsive	Encouraged	Smart
Stupid	Good	Communication
Strong	Worried	Nature
Dream	Small	Sad
Unsexy	Grief	Great
Passionate	Frustrated	Outgoing
Bad	Alive	Free
Optimistic	Excited	Shame
Miserable	Embarrassed	Insulted
Happy	Reading	Book
Suspicious	Unpleasant	Glad
Inferior	Unsatisfied	Guilt
Confused	Shy	Joyful
Powerless	Peaceful	Dumb
Sensitive		

The Thought-Feeling Formula is [I think X] + [I feel Y about that].

Take the example, "I feel like you don't care about me," and plug it into the Thought-Feeling Formula below. Note that in this example, you'll have to pretend how someone saying this might be feeling.

[I think _____ _____ _____   _____ _____ _____ _____   _____ _____ _____ _____

_____ _____ _____ _____ _____   _____ _____]

+

[I feel _____ about that].

Now, consider three situations in your own life where you would want to say "I feel like . . ." For example, "I feel like this isn't working," "I feel like I want more," or "I feel like you're being rude." Take some time to reflect upon your own life and write down three scenarios.

1. I feel like _____

_____

2. I feel like _____

_____

3. I feel like _____

_____

Next, plug your three "I feel like . . ." statements into the Thought-Feeling Formula. Extra space is available on the next page in case the lines on this page aren't sufficient.

[I think _____]

+

[I feel _____ about that].

[I think _____]

+

[I feel _____ about that].

[I think _____]

+

[I feel _____ about that].

Now, speak what you've written in your formulas aloud as a complete sentence. As an example, "I feel like you don't care about me" became [I think you don't care about me] + [I feel sad and frustrated about that] with the formula. Then, speaking it aloud in one complete sentence becomes, "I think you don't care about me, and I feel sad and frustrated about that." Write your three complete sentences out below and then speak them aloud. There's extra space on the next page if the lines on this page aren't sufficient.

I think _____

_____

and I feel _____ about that.

I think _____

_____

and I feel _____ about that.

I think _____

_____

and I feel _____ about that.

If you and your partner are new to consciously communicating, it could be a bit of a shock to your partner if you just walked up and said, "I think you don't care about me, and I feel frustrated about that." This is where a Soft Startup is useful.

The Gottman Institute coined the term, and it's a sentence or phrase that prepares your partner for the challenging conversation you're about to engage in. Put a checkmark (✓) next to the sentences below that would be considered a Soft Startup and an X (**x**) next to the ones that would not be considered a Soft Startup.

Hey, come here, I have to talk to you.

Do you have some time to talk in a few minutes?

Sit down. I want to talk to you.

I have something I want to share, but it's a difficult conversation for me. Can we sit down to talk about it?

I wanted to share my feelings about something. You might not see it the same way, and that's okay, but I want to get out what I have to say and then you can share your perspective once I'm finished. Does that sound okay?

I have something to say, but are you actually going to listen for once in your life?

Hey, I have something I want to share my perspective on. And then I want to hear your perspective.

I'm about to say something but you're probably just going to not care like you always do.

I'd like to talk about something on my mind. I think it's important. When would be a good time for you today?

When you share your thoughts and feelings from the previous exercise with your partner, don't forget to use one of the Soft Startup options.

Communication Technique #6
"I Feel"
Instead of saying, "You make me feel," say, "I feel . . ."

Multiple Choice: Choose all that apply

Saying "You made me feel . . ." or "That makes me feel . . ." is an excellent way to:

A. Communicate your feelings to your partner

B. Remove the possibility of emotional stability from your life

C. Give away your power

D. Build more trust with your partner

E. Covertly attack your partner

F. Miss out on an opportunity for deeper emotional healing for yourself

Can you identify an event or experience from your childhood that "sleeps" inside of you and awakens only when your partner says certain trigger words or does certain trigger actions? Hint: Whenever you're off-the-charts angry, completely shutting down, or emotionally triggered above and beyond a level commensurate with what your partner said or did, this is an indication of a sleeping emotional wound awakening. Reflect and write below (and onto the next page if needed) about your sleeping emotional wounds that awaken when interacting with your partner.

_____

_____

_____

_____

Fill in the Blank

Your partner's words and actions can _____ _____ _____ _____ _____ _____ you of your preexisting

feelings, but they can't _____ _____ _____ _____ _____ _____ feelings in you.

Multiple Choice: Choose all that apply

Which are proper apologies?

    A. I'm sorry you feel upset.

    B. I'm sorry I made you upset.

    C. I'm sorry for saying mean things. That was wrong of me.

    D. I'm sorry you're upset with me.

    E. I'm sorry for doing that. It's on me and it wasn't okay.

Reword the following sentences using "I feel . . ."

You make me so angry.

_____

_____

When you talk to me like that, it makes me frustrated and sad.

_____

_____

You make me nuts!

_____

_____

You piss me off so much!

_____

_____

You made me sad for months because of what you did.

_____

_____

Now, consider a situation with your partner when you either blurted out or wanted to blurt out, "You make me [ ]!" and reframe the phrase below using "I feel . . ."

_____

_____

_____

_____

PART III
When You've Made a Mistake

Fill in the Blank

I will make _____ _____ _____ _____ _____ _____ _____ _____ in my relationship.

When I make a _____ _____ _____ _____ _____ _____ _____ in my relationship,

it's important that I properly _____ _____ _____ _____ _____ _____ _____ _____ _____ instead of

glossing over it, expecting my partner to just get over it, or trying make amends purely through actions because I'm too afraid/embarrassed/ashamed to directly acknowledge when I've made

a _____ _____ _____ _____ _____ _____ _____.

Communication Technique #7
"I Was Wrong"
Instead of saying, "Look what you made me do," say, "I was wrong."

Multiple Choice: Choose the best answer

If you've said or done something you recognize as hurtful, avoid thinking of the issue as "in the past" until you've:

A. Gotten down on your knees and begged the person for another chance.

B. Explained why you did it or said it.

C. Given your partner 24 hours to process things and cool off.

D. Acknowledged that your words or actions were wrong.

True or False

If someone forgives you, it also means they have to trust you again, otherwise it isn't true forgiveness.
True / False

Rebuilding trust after a hurt can often be as simple as acknowledging to your partner that you understand what you did was wrong and saying you're sorry. Personally reflect on what saying "I was wrong" brings up for you. Is it hard for you to say? Does it mean your entire existence is wrong rather than just your isolated words or actions? Do you feel embarrassment or shame? Would you rather do anything, even swim across the Pacific Ocean and back, rather than say those words? Where did you learn to avoid verbally acknowledging when you've done something wrong? Write your reflections on this subject below and onto the next page.

_____

_____

_____

Reflect on whether you and your partner are trying to hang on to the honeymoon phase of your relationship. Do you openly speak to one another about issues? Do you sweep issues and concerns under the rug in the name of not disturbing the peace or keeping up an external image of getting along perfectly? What issues have you been sweeping under the rug that need to be discussed?

_____

_____

_____

_____

_____

_____

_____

_____

_____

_____

_____

_____

Is there something hurtful you said or did in the past that hasn't yet been acknowledged in the form of "I was wrong" and "I'm sorry"? You might be letting your partner know you're sorry through your actions, and actions are vitally important. But if you haven't verbally acknowledged that you understand what you said or did was wrong, then your partner might be wondering if you realize the harm of your words or actions. Or, your partner may think you're being more kind out of guilt or fear, and not because you authentically understand that what you said or did was wrong. "But they should just know because I'm acting differently!" No, no—it's time to stop the assuming, shoulding, and avoiding difficult verbal interactions. Reflect below on the areas where you haven't yet verbally acknowledged your hurtful words or actions. And remember, doing something wrong means you made a mistake at a given point in time—it doesn't mean your entire existence is a mistake.

_____

_____

_____

_____

_____

_____

_____

_____

_____

_____

Since trust was mentioned in one of the reflection questions related to this communication technique, keep in mind that trust is not an all-or-nothing characteristic in relationships. People tend to become very upset if they're not trusted, but the truth is that trust can be present in some areas while not present in other areas. For example, your partner might trust you'll be there when you say you will and that you're always available to help out with chores or projects, but they may not trust you to be able to have difficult conversations.

Rather than go on a tirade of telling your partner how much you do and how could they dare not trust you, understand that trust is situational. Instead of becoming immediately defensive, which is so common because everybody wants to view themselves as trustworthy (and will therefore defend their trustworthiness to the bitter end), get curious.

Get curious about why your partner doesn't trust you in a specific area. They might tell you about a situation that happened, and then you might get defensive and say, "Well I only did that one time. Have I ever done it again?" Don't do this, because one slice with a sword is enough to cause a long-term injury. Instead, say, "I know that must have been really painful, and you have a right to take as long as you need to work through it."

In your relationship, there are going to be areas where trust is strong and other areas where trust is weak or nonexistent. In the words of Kevin Malone from *The Office*, "It's only human natural."

*If you're not familiar with *The Office* but want to understand the reference:
https://getyarn.io/yarn-clip/fce61a5f-99c0-4917-97f6-b7a96e2c4237.
Or simply type "Kevin Malone human natural" into Google and look for the three-second-long "Yarn" video.

Therefore, don't pressure your partner to one hundred percent trust you in all areas.

In what areas do you trust your partner based on their past words and actions? In what areas don't you trust your partner based on their past words and actions?

_____

_____

_____

_____

_____

In what areas can your partner trust you based on your past words and actions? In what areas might your partner have difficulty trusting you based on your past words and actions? Consider it from their perspective, not from your own. Remember, a change in your relationship is going to require deeper self-honesty than you've ever before engaged in.

_____

_____

_____

_____

_____

_____

_____

_____

_____

_____

_____

Communication Technique #8
"~~I Apologize~~" "I'm Sorry"
Instead of saying, "I apologize," say, "I'm sorry."

Do you apologize to keep the peace, even if you haven't done something wrong? Reflect below on the short-term and long-term effects apologizing to keep the peace has had on the quality of your relationship.

_____

_____

_____

_____

_____

_____

_____

_____

_____

Do you avoid apologizing when you've done something wrong, instead opting to wait a little while and then acting like everything's okay and the argument never happened? Reflect below on the short-term and long-term effects acting like the argument never happened has had on your relationship.

_____

_____

_____

_____

_____

_____

_____

_____

_____

_____

_____

_____

Have you chosen to avoid the discomfort of apologizing after you've said or done something hurtful? Reflect below on the specific discomfort(s) you're avoiding by choosing to not apologize. As common examples, people want to avoid feelings of embarrassment and shame. You could also be avoiding the difficulty of a hard conversation, the fear of how your partner will respond, or the fear of not knowing how to handle yourself if your partner is upset with you. Reflect on the exact discomforts you're avoiding when you choose to not apologize. Don't be general, be specific.

_____

PART IV
Responding to Your Partner's Feelings

How you respond to your partner's feelings makes a huge difference. In this section, you'll be working on responding in ways that promote trust and emotional safety within the relationship.

Communication Technique #9
"It's Great You're Letting This Out"
Instead of saying, "Don't cry," say, "It's great you're letting this out."

Multiple Choice: Choose all that apply

Crying is:

    A. A sign of weakness.

    B. Unnatural

    C. Something that happens only if someone has something seriously wrong with them

    D. Human

    E. A sign of fragility

    F. Part of life

    G. Something that happens only during psychotic episodes and mental breakdowns

    H. A bad sign

    I. Something that needs to be stopped as soon as possible

    J. An organic response to loss

    K. A healthy way to release and integrate grief

Appropriate responses to my partner crying include:

    A. Trying to make them laugh

    B. Offering to do their favorite activity

    C. Sitting there and being present

    D. Explaining why they should stop crying

    E. Placing a hand on their shoulder, back, or thigh

    F. Offering to plan a night out doing all their favorite things

When their partners are upset and crying, most people respond by either, a) trying to fix the problem, or b) trying to get them to stop crying. How do you normally respond if your partner is crying? Reflect on past instances and remember how you responded. But don't stop there. Go deeper and reflect upon why you responded that way. What beliefs and previous life experiences drove you to respond the way you did?

_____

_____

_____

_____

_____

_____

_____

_____

_____

_____

_____

_____

Are you uncomfortable when someone else is upset and crying? Do you have an overwhelming sense of wanting to fix their pain? Do you have anxiety about what to do or how to respond? Reflect below on what happens inside yourself when someone else is crying. What sensations come up? What feelings? What beliefs about crying do you hold? What pressures do you place on yourself and the other person? Be specific.

_____

_____

_____

_____

_____

_____

_____

_____

_____

_____

_____

Growing up, what were the messages you received about emotional expression? For example, maybe certain emotions were allowed while others weren't. Or, maybe one parent used crying to propagate a victim role instead of using it to express grief due to loss. What were the specific messages you learned about emotional expression by your family or caregivers?

_____

_____

_____

_____

_____

_____

_____

_____

_____

_____

_____

_____

Do you allow yourself to grieve losses? If not, the built-up energy over the unexpressed grief can show up as tension in your relationship. Which losses do you need to take time to grieve? Loss can be anything from the passing of a loved one, losing a car you loved, losing a certain physical function, moving away from family and friends, losing a job you loved, and so on. Don't judge them as "too small" to be worthy of grieving. Some losses may require more time to fully grieve while others need just a few moments, but all losses are worthy of being grieved. As you enter into grieving your losses, keep in mind that successfully grieving means feeling the pain of the loss, not engaging in self-pity.

_____

_____

_____

_____

_____

_____

_____

_____

_____

_____

Communication Technique #10
Let Them Be Upset with You
Instead of saying, "Don't be upset with me," say,
"You can be upset with me as long as you want."

Reflect on how you feel when your partner is upset with you. You may have never reflected upon this because it's so uncomfortable for you when they're upset with you. You might immediately go into fixing mode, avoiding mode, defending mode, or attack-mode. Put all of that aside, and just sit with the internal feelings that come up for you when your partner is upset with you. Let's not take this to extremes, though. We're not talking about partners who are physically abusive or threatening physical violence. In this exercise, we're talking about situations when your partner is emotionally upset with you, and how your internal psychological and emotional landscape reacts.

To help you reflect on this, consider the following:

What does it mean about me if my partner is upset with me?

What physiological feelings come up for me?

What emotions inside are too overwhelming to sit with pertaining to my partner being upset?

What beliefs do I have about what it means for our relationship if one of us is upset with the other?

Reflect below and on the next page.

_____

_____

_____

_____

_____

Underlying messages aren't directly stated; they're implied. Recognizing the underlying messages in your statements will help you and your partner create clean and clear communication.

Identify the underlying messages within the following statements and write them out.

Even a six-year-old could figure out how to use this program. _____

_____

Please don't be mad at me. _____

_____

Why do you find it necessary to not tell me things? _____

_____

Next, think back to some of the statements you've made either while you were upset or while your partner was upset. Looking back, what underlying messages can you now identify in your statements that you didn't notice were present at the time?

_____

_____

_____

_____

_____

_____

When working through upset feelings, either yours toward your partner or theirs toward you, which questions below are useful? Which questions are unhelpful?

Check (✓) the useful questions and cross out the unhelpful ones.

Why do I feel this way?

How can I get you to stop being mad at me?

What was going through your head when this happened?

What's it going to take for them to drop this conversation?

What was your intention?

How can I turn this around and put it back on them?

What was my intention or motive for saying or doing what I did?

Have I ever felt this way before—while growing up or in another relationship?

What overwhelming feelings am I experiencing?

How can I express and work through these feelings in a healthy way?

How am I internally responding (i.e., emotions, beliefs, automatic thoughts) in this moment?

Can you think of other useful questions to ask yourself in these situations? Can you identify other unhelpful questions?

_____

_____

_____

_____

_____

Communication Technique #11
Set a Boundary
Instead of meeting disrespect with more disrespect, set a boundary.

True or False

"Would you stop calling me needy?" is a boundary. True / False

"Never, ever call me dumb again," is a boundary. True / False

"I'm asking you calmly, please let me know if you're going to be late," is a boundary. True / False

"If you call me stupid again, I'm not speaking to you for the next 24 hours," is a boundary. True / False

"Do it again and see what happens," is a boundary. True / False

Fill in the Blank

Boundaries have a _____% success rate.

A boundary is only a boundary when it involves something you have

_____ _____ _____ _____ _____ _____ _____ over.

Multiple Choice: Choose all that apply

Boundaries are not:

    A. Threats

    B. Demands

    C. Requests

Have you ever set a boundary with someone who was treating you poorly only to take it back thereafter? Reflect on what internal dynamics within yourself drove you to take it back. In other words, an internal feeling arose that eventually manifested as the thought, "I need to take back my boundary." Therefore, don't necessarily reflect on your intellectual reasoning for taking it back. Instead, reflect on the internal feeling that drove you to develop the intellectual reasoning.

_____

_____

_____

_____

_____

_____

_____

_____

_____

_____

_____

_____

The basic formula for communicating a boundary is [If X] + [Then Y]. As an example, if your partner insults you by calling you a name, the boundary format would look like:

[If you don't apologize for calling me that name within the next hour]
+
[Then I'm going to remove myself from conversing with you for 24 hours]

Made into a complete sentence, it would be, "If you don't apologize for calling me that name in the next hour, then I'm going to remove myself from conversing with you for 24 hours."

Consider four situations and write them out in the format described above. Remember to use a consequence that matches the behavior. For two of the situations, consider boundaries you would set with your partner. These could be boundaries that were needed in that past or that might be needed sometime in the near future. For the other two situations, consider boundaries your partner would set with you. Yes, you read that correctly. It's important that you're able to self-reflect honestly enough to identify your behaviors that aren't healthy for the relationship.

_____

_____

_____

_____

_____

_____

_____

Have you and your partner mutually agreed that name-calling, shaming, disrespect, and insults have no place in your relationship? If not, this is an important conversation to have. While you hope it doesn't happen, there's still a chance one of you slips from time to time in this area. Have a conversation together about refraining from these verbal behaviors so that if and when it comes up, neither person is surprised when it's handled by setting a boundary if there isn't an immediate ownership of responsibility and apology. Below, write about how you'll bring this subject up to your partner and what you'd like to get across during the conversation.

_____

_____

_____

_____

_____

_____

_____

_____

_____

_____

Boundaries are a complex subject. When adding in potential misunderstandings and misinterpretations, boundaries can be filled with more gray areas than black or white. Therefore, I think a few additional notes on boundaries are in order.

First, you must stop viewing your relationship as a competition. Who's going to win out? The answer: Nobody. There's not a winner because a winner means there's a loser. And if there's someone who loses, then the entire relationship loses. Remember to view it as what's good for the relationship, not necessarily for this individual or that individual. With that mindset, you can be glad for your partner when they set an appropriate boundary with you. This isn't a one-way street where you get to set boundaries and your partner doesn't. Embrace deep self-honesty and recognize where you've said or done something hurtful. If your partner addresses those areas with a boundary, especially if you didn't take accountability for it, be glad, because it's good for the overall relationship.

Related to that is recognizing your own contribution to the issue. Just because your partner committed a hurtful deed doesn't give you a free pass to call them names and constantly blame them. They may have done something hurtful, but are you responding in a calm, clean and clear way? Or have you been triggered into your own unhealthy behaviors? Don't use your partner as a black sheep, thinking you don't have to take responsibility for your words or actions because their negative behavior justifies your negative behavior. It's understood that you're hurting, and addressing your hurt is important. However, being hurt doesn't afford a pass to shame or insult someone else. Remember, the purpose of a boundary is to meet disrespect with respect.

Lastly but not least importantly, use resources to determine boundaries that need to be set. Some situations are clear, such as name-calling or throwing a dangerous object like a piece of glass that shatters all over the place. Other areas aren't so clear. In these cases, consult multiple objective third parties. If all your therapist does is validate but never challenge you, they're probably not objective. They're probably projecting their own wounded areas onto you, and therefore are unable to be objective with you. Seek mentors, therapists, coaches, and friends who care more about truth and reality in any given situation than building up your ego. Journal about the situation. Seek truth at all costs, even if it's not pleasing or pleasant.

Below, reflect on your feelings and thoughts about boundaries.

_____

_____

_____

_____

_____

Communication Technique #12
"I'm Happy You Want to Improve"
Instead of viewing it as a personal attack,
view it as a good thing they want to improve the relationship.

Is it okay with you if your partner brings up issues about you or your relationship? Do you have a sense of openness and a genuine interest in exploring these issues? Or, do you often find yourself wanting to be defensive? Do you have a sense of having to give reasons for your "goodness"? Do you take it as an attack on you as an entire person rather than an isolated issue? Reflect below on how you typically respond when your partner brings up issues about you or your relationship.

_____

_____

_____

_____

_____

_____

_____

_____

_____

Fill in the Blank

Every relationship has ____ ____ ____ ____ ____ ____ ____ ____ ____ ____ and

areas of ____ ____ ____ ____ ____ ____.

Do you proactively seek out and discuss growth areas about yourself and your relationship with your partner? Or, do you tend more toward the side of not giving such areas much thought until it's brought up by your partner? Reflect below on how you typically show up in this area.

_____

_____

_____

_____

_____

_____

_____

_____

_____

Fill in the Blank

Multiple Choice: Choose all that apply

"My partner should just love me for who I am and never bring up any issues about me or the relationship" is a:

A.   Healthy perspective

B.   Reasonable viewpoint and totally attainable

C.   Belief that comes from an unhealed inner child

D.   Fantasy

Can you differentiate between something that has no truth to it and something that has truth to it but was brought up in a less-than-ideal way? In other words, just because your partner doesn't do a good job phrasing or wording something doesn't mean there's no truth to it. Don't write them off completely in these cases. Instead, address the fact that you don't like their tone or use of disrespectful words, but you'd still like to explore the overall issue and see if there's any truth to what they're saying. Handle it as two separate situations. This is an advanced relationship skill.

As an example, your partner might say, "You look like an idiot when you act that way." In response, you can say, "I'd like an apology for using the word idiot at me. But I'm also open to exploring my behavior and examining whether there's anything I can address from my end." Don't let your partner speak disrespectfully to you, but also don't completely write off their concerns just because there's a flaw in how they're presenting it.

Reflect below on a time when you brought something up in a less-than-ideal way. Did the fact that it was brought up poorly by you make the issue less real? Next, reflect on a time when you wrote your partner off even though there was some truth in what they were saying.

_____

_____

_____

_____

_____

Fill in the Blank

Instead of viewing yourself as good or bad, great or terrible, begin viewing yourself as

_____ _____ _____ _____ _____ in some areas and in need of _____ _____ _____ _____ _____ _____

in other areas.

Put a mark through the toxic beliefs below and circle the healthy beliefs.

A. I'm either a good partner or a bad one. Period.

B. I either meet all of my partner's needs, or I meet none of them.

C. I bring a lot to this relationship, and I also have areas of growth I need to address.

D. If my partner doesn't gush over every single part of me, it means they think I'm terrible.

E. My partner likes many things about me, and there are also areas they'd like me to improve.

F. My partner bringing up an issue about me or the relationship means they don't like me and I'm not good enough.

G. My partner bringing up an issue about me or the relationship means they care so much about the relationship that they want to put energy into growing and healing it.

Fill in the Blank

All relationships _____ _____ _____ _____ _____ _____. It's your choice whether your relationship

_____ _____ _____ _____ _____ _____ _____ in a conscious, proactive way, or in an unconscious way.

Communication Technique #13
Examine Both Sides
Instead of blaming, examine both sides of the situation.

When telling someone else about your relationship problems—like a friend, mentor, therapist, group, etc.—do you paint a picture of yourself as innocent and your partner as the at-fault party? Think back to therapy sessions, venting sessions with friends, or other discussions, but this time fill in the blanks with the parts about yourself you left out when telling the other person about the situation. What things did you do or say that you left out of the picture you painted for the other person?

_____

_____

_____

_____

_____

_____

_____

_____

_____

_____

Do you tend to think in either/or, black or white ways? Next time you and your partner have a disagreement, how can you remind yourself that one person having a legitimate viewpoint doesn't automatically make the other person's viewpoint invalid? Write down below how you'll remind yourself of this the next time a disagreement arises. Potential options could be using a journal, notes on your phone, sticky notes, talking about it in-depth with your therapist, and so on. Come up with a plan of action for when the time comes so you don't fall into the same pattern.

_____

_____

_____

_____

_____

_____

_____

_____

_____

_____

_____

Can you examine your role in a situation without beating yourself up mentally and emotionally? What happens inside yourself mentally and emotionally when you realize you're at fault for something? What happens inside yourself if you admit you were wrong? Explore your internal dynamics pertaining to these situations below.

_____

_____

_____

_____

_____

_____

_____

_____

_____

_____

_____

_____

Practice holding your partner **and** yourself accountable by using sentences with the phrase "in addition". For example, "I don't like the tone you used with me; in addition, I acknowledge that I was rolling my eyes which can be harmful to our relationship." Below, reflect on past situations and situations you suspect might come up again down the road, and practice addressing the situations using the phrase "in addition".

_____

_____

_____

_____

_____

_____

_____

_____

_____

_____

_____

Fill in the Blank

Refusing to examine your contributing factors in relationship issues means you are seeking a

_____ _____ _____ _____ _____ _____ - _____ _____ _____ _____ _____ dynamic, and within that

dynamic, you are the _____ _____ _____ _____ _____. (Psychologically and emotionally speaking, that is.)

Summary

Fill in the Blank

_____ _____ _____ _____ _____ _____ _____ _____ _____ struggles with communication, so don't

beat yourself up.

Multiple Choice: Choose all that apply

Unhealthy communication looks like:

    A.   Deflecting issues

    B.   Speaking directly yet respectfully

    C.   Avoiding issues

    D.   Blaming

    E.   Getting curious about the situation

    F.   Not examining your role in the situation

Healthy communication looks like:

    A.   Actively working through issues

    B.   Only describing how the other person is doing or saying wrong or hurtful things

    C.   Squarely facing difficult issues and conversations

    D.   Evading conversations and hoping the issues will just go away

    E.   Speaking respectfully without sacrificing what you mean to say

    F.   Utilizing a both/and attitude rather than an either/or attitude

Fill in the Blank

A novice communicator expects a

_____ _____ _____ _____ _____ _____ _____ _____ - _____ _____ _____ _____ process when

communicating.

A seasoned communicator knows there will be dozens of

_____ _____ _____ _____ _____ _____ _____ _____ _____ _____ _____ along the way.

You'll be happier when you forget how things "_____ _____ _____ _____ _____ _____" be and begin

addressing situations as they are.

Moving Forward

I hope this workbook has inspired you to make self-reflection a way of life. This workbook was intended to encourage you to reflect on difficult areas within yourself that affect how you show up in your relationship. It's not meant to fix your relationship once and for all, but to teach you how to deeply self-reflect so you can use the skill for years to come. Stressors and challenges will continue to arise—that's not even a question. If you're asking yourself, "So is everything going to be smooth sailing and only smooth sailing moving forward?" the answer is no. Challenges will arise in your relationship because you are two different people who see the world through two different sets of eyes.

The key isn't whether or not your relationship is all smooth sailing. The key is this: Will you approach challenges, difficult times, and disagreements through a lens of self-reflection?

If you do, you'll grow closer and closer with each challenge you work through together. If you don't, blame and finger-pointing will create a wider and wider chasm between the two of you.

It's important to note here that while challenges won't go away, you'll constantly trade up. What I mean by that is if you maintain an attitude of self-reflection throughout all of your relationship challenges, you'll both be learning and growing psychologically and emotionally. Therefore, because you'll be psychologically and emotionally more mature with each passing month and year, certain areas that were once issues will become non-issues. For example, name-calling will never again be an issue because you've grown beyond the level of development a person has to be stuck in to call their partner names. Or, as another example, keeping your word will become a way of life and not something you do just on occasion. You'll grow out of the issues and challenges that were in alignment with your former stage of emotional and psychological development. From there, new challenges that are aligned with your new stage of development will arise. Eventually, you may not even see them as challenges. They're just the next growth opportunity. As my late mentor, Ron, often said, "AFGO." Another f*ck!ng growth opportunity.

With each growth opportunity, you'll self-reflect, learn, apply, and then mature into the next stage of emotional and psychological development.

Did you know your body is constantly changing? Fuel is being burned, used, and disposed of, old cells are being replaced with new ones, and there's constant movement in your bloodstream. There's no such thing as a stagnant body. There's also no such thing as a stagnant personality. Emotions come and go and experiences impact how you see yourself and others. The difference is whether you'll remain unconscious or become conscious of the emotional and psychological movement within you day to day, month to month, year to year.

Will you and your partner commit to a joint effort in remaining self-aware and conscious going forward? Or, will you go back to sleep after you close this workbook? If you both continue self-reflecting as a way of life, you'll both have the pleasure of seeing one another grow and blossom, and you'll be more deeply connected for it.

One Last Thing

If you found this workbook useful, will you leave a review on Amazon? Don't worry—it doesn't have to be a long review. Just a sentence or two describing what you found useful about the workbook is plenty.

Leaving a review is simple and takes less than a minute to complete:

First, go to this workbook's product page on Amazon.

Second, click on the "Write a customer review" or "Write a review" button.

Third, choose a star rating.

Fourth, write a sentence or two about what was most helpful to you.

That's all it takes.

Read Next

Learn to Love Yourself Again
A Step-by-Step Guide to Conquer Self-Hatred, Ditch Self-Loathing, & Cultivate Self-Compassion
Self-love isn't selfish. It's only with self-love that you can bring the best version of yourself to the world. So, dig in and learn to love yourself. As one reviewer wrote, this book helped her break out of her mental prison.

Healing Your Inner Critic
5 Keys to Transforming Shame & Experiencing Inner Freedom
Most people think you have to "fight" your inner critic to get it to quiet down. That never works, but there is a way that *does* work. One reviewer wrote, "I've finally been able to stop blaming/shaming myself. A life changing read."

Outsmart Negative Thinking
Simple Mindfulness Methods to Control Negative Thoughts, Stop Anxiety, & Finally Experience Happiness
In the martial art of Judo, you don't necessarily stop your opponent. Your opponent keeps on moving while you use their momentum against them. Stop trying to stop your negative thinking. Take another approach, a gentler approach that works, instead. As one reviewer puts it, "If your mind won't shut up, get it."

Answer Key

Page 11 Answers

You shouldn't fold the laundry like that. You should fold it like this. → I would like you to fold the laundry like this.

You shouldn't leave the dishes in the sink. You should wash them right away. → I would like you to wash your dishes right away after using them.

You should do more to help around the house. → I would like more help around the house.

Page 12 Answers

You shouldn't wait until your tank is on E to fill it up. → I would like you to get gas before the tank is all the way on E because I worry about you getting stuck somewhere.

You should workout more often. → I would like you to workout more often because I'm worried about your health.

You should get help. → I would like to see you talk to someone because I'm concerned for your mental health and want you to feel happier.

You shouldn't use the word "should." → I would like you to rephrase your sentences instead of using the word "should," because the word should implies there's something wrong with a person if they don't do the thing you're telling them they should do.

You should forgive that person. → I would like to see you forgive that person, not for their benefit, but for your own well-being because I see that not forgiving them is causing you a lot of stress and bitterness inside yourself.

Page 17 Answers

<u>Feelings</u> are never invalid, but <u>reasons</u> for the <u>feelings</u> can be discussed, examined, and evaluated.

Multiple Choice: Choose the best answer

If I'm angry or overwhelmed in a discussion and I take a break from the discussion to process my feelings, who's responsibility is it to reengage with the conversation?

   A. My partner's

   B. My child's, who plays a peacekeeper/fixer/mediator role

   C. Anyone but me

   D. Oh God, please, not me

 E. Mine

What is your responsibility?

   A. How another adult behaves

   B. The harmful words of another adult

   C. Your feelings pertaining to any given situation

Page 22 Answers

I'm not actually waiting for the right time to communicate. I'm waiting for the <u>fear</u> and <u>anxiety</u> about <u>communicating</u> to go away.

Page 24 Answers

A feeling isn't a <u>thought</u> and a <u>thought</u> isn't a feeling.

Page 25 Answers

Multiple Choice: Choose the best answer

Which of these statements accurately separates thoughts from feelings?

    A. I feel it would be best to not go to this event.

    B. I feel like it wouldn't be a good idea to go to this event.

    C. I'm not feeling like going to this event.

    (D.) None of the above.

*In all three sentences, the word *feel* or *feeling* is used, but there isn't a feeling actually identified.

A thought is something you experience in the form of <u>words</u> and <u>images</u>.

A feeling is something you experience in your <u>body</u> in the form of physiological <u>sensations</u>.

Which of the following are feelings? Which are descriptive words of feelings? Which are neither? Put a checkmark next to the feelings (✓), a dot next to the descriptive words of feelings (•), and an X (**x**) next to those that are neither.

✓Fear	•Rejected	✓Terror
x Therapy	•Paranoid	•Less than
x Sky	•Abandoned	✓Anger
•Empty	•Ugly	•Confident
✓Rage	**x** Mountains	•Powerful
✓Humiliated	•Unreliable	✓Anxiety
•Impulsive	•Encouraged	•Smart
•Stupid	•Good	**x** Communication
•Strong	✓Worried	**x** Nature
x Dream	•Small	✓Sad
•Unsexy	✓Grief	•Great
•Passionate	✓Frustrated	•Outgoing
•Bad	•Alive	•Free
•Optimistic	✓Excited	✓Shame
•Miserable	✓Embarrassed	•Insulted
✓Happy	**x** Reading	**x** Book
•Suspicious	•Unpleasant	✓Glad
•Inferior	•Unsatisfied	✓Guilt
•Confused	•Shy	✓Joyful
•Powerless	✓Peaceful	•Dumb
•Sensitive		

Page 27 Answers

Take the example, "I feel like you don't care about me," and plug it into the Thought-Feeling Formula below. Note that in this example, you'll have to pretend how someone saying this might be feeling.

[I think <u>you don't care about me</u>] **+** [I feel <u>sad</u> about that].

Page 32 Answers

Put a checkmark (✓) next to the sentences below that would be considered a Soft Startup and an X (**x**) next to the ones that wouldn't be considered a Soft Startup.

x Hey, come here, I have to talk to you.

✓ Do you have some time to talk in a few minutes?

x Sit down. I want to talk to you.

✓ I have something I want to share, but it's a difficult conversation for me. Can we sit down to talk about it?

✓ I wanted to share my feelings about something. You might not see it the same way, and that's okay, but I want to get out what I have to say and then you can share your perspective once I'm finished. Does that sound okay?

x I have something to say, but are you actually going to listen for once in your life?

✓ Hey, I have something I want to share my perspective on. And then I want to hear your perspective.

x I'm about to say something but you're probably just going to not care like you always do.

✓ I'd like to talk about something on my mind. I think it's important. When would be a good time for you today?

Multiple Choice: Choose all that apply

Saying "You made me feel . . ." or "That makes me feel . . ." is an excellent way to:

A. Communicate your feelings to your partner

B. Remove the possibility of emotional stability from your life

C. Give away your power

D. Build more trust with your partner

E. Covertly attack your partner

F. Miss out on an opportunity for deeper emotional healing for yourself

Page 35 Answers

Fill in the Blank

Your partner's words and actions can <u>remind</u> you of your preexisting feelings, but they can't <u>create</u> feelings in you.

Multiple Choice: Choose all that apply

Which are proper apologies?

    A. I'm sorry you feel upset.

    B. I'm sorry I made you upset.

    (C.) I'm sorry for saying mean things. That was wrong of me.

    D. I'm sorry you're upset with me.

    (E.) I'm sorry for doing that. It's on me and it wasn't okay.

Page 35 and 36 Answers

35

Reword the following sentences using "I feel . . ."

You make me so angry. → I feel so angry when you say/do that.

When you talk to me like that, it makes me frustrated and sad. → When you talk to me like that, I feel frustrated and sad.

36

You make me nuts! → When you do those things/say those things, I feel so much anxiety/fear/anger/frustration/sadness that I'm to the point of being overwhelmed by it.

You piss me off so much! → I'm feeling angry to the point that I need a break from our interaction for 20 minutes/30 minutes/an hour. After that amount of time I'll come back to finish our conversation.

You made me sad for months because of what you did. → After you said/did that, I felt sad for months.

Page 37 Answers

I will make <u>mistakes</u> in my relationship. When I make a <u>mistake</u> in my relationship, it's important that I properly <u>apologize</u> instead of glossing over it, expecting my partner to just get over it, or trying make amends purely through actions because I'm too afraid/embarrassed/ashamed to directly acknowledge when I've made a <u>mistake</u>.

Page 38 Answers

Multiple Choice: Choose the best answer

If you've said or done something you recognize as hurtful, avoid thinking of the issue as "in the past" until you've:

    A. Gotten down on your knees and begged the person for another chance.

    B. Explained why you did it or said it.

    C. Given your partner 24 hours to process things and cool off.

    (D.) Acknowledged that your words or actions were wrong.

If someone forgives you, it also means they have to trust you again, otherwise it isn't true forgiveness.
True (False)

Multiple Choice: Choose all that apply

Crying is:

    A. A sign of weakness

    B. Unnatural

    C. Something that happens only if someone has something seriously wrong with them

    (D.) Human

    E. A sign of fragility

    (F.) Part of life

    G. Something that happens only during psychotic episodes and mental breakdowns

    H. A bad sign

    I. Something that needs to be stopped as soon as possible

    (J.) An organic response to loss

    (K.) A healthy way to release and integrate grief

Appropriate responses to my partner crying include:

    A. Trying to make them laugh

    B. Offering to do their favorite activity

    (C.) Sitting there and being present

    D. Explaining why they should stop crying

    (E.) Placing a hand on their shoulder, back, or thigh

    F. Offering to plan a night out doing all their favorite things

Page 57 Answers

Even a six-year-old could figure out how to use this program.
Underlying Message: You're dumber/less intelligent than a six-year-old.

Please don't be mad at me.
Underlying Message: Your feelings of anger aren't okay.

Why do you find it necessary to not tell me things?
Underlying Message: You purposely didn't tell me about this.

Page 58 Answers

When working through upset feelings, either yours toward your partner or theirs toward you, which questions below are useful? Which questions are unhelpful?

Check (✓) the useful questions and cross out the unhelpful ones.

✓ Why do I feel this way?

~~How can I get you to stop being mad at me?~~

✓ What was going through your head when this happened?
*Note that this is useful when used as a genuine question and not in a sarcastic "What were you thinking?" manner.

~~What's it going to take for them to drop this conversation?~~

✓ What was your intention?

~~How can I turn this around and put it back on them?~~

✓ What was my intention or motive for saying or doing what I did?

✓ Have I ever felt this way before—while growing up or in another relationship?

✓ What overwhelming feelings am I experiencing?

✓ How can I express and work through these feelings in a healthy way?

✓ How am I internally responding (i.e., emotions, beliefs, automatic thoughts) in this moment?

Page 59 Answers

True or False

"Would you stop calling me needy?" is a boundary. True /(False)

   *It's a request, not a boundary. You have no control over whether they call you needy.

"Never, ever call me dumb again," is a boundary. True /(False)

   *Not a boundary, as you have no control over whether they call you this name again.

"I'm asking you calmly, please let me know if you're going to be late," is a boundary. True /(False)

   *Not a boundary, a request. You have no control over them letting you know.

"If you call me stupid again, I'm not speaking to you for the next 24 hours."(True)/ False

   *This is a boundary because you have complete control over whether you speak to them for the next 24 hours if they call you stupid again.

"Do it again and see what happens," is a boundary. True /(False)

   *Not a boundary, a threat. You have no control over whether they do it again.

Fill in the Blank

Boundaries have a <u>100%</u> success rate.

A boundary is only a boundary when it involves something you have <u>control</u> over.

Multiple Choice: Choose all that apply

Boundaries are not:

(A.) Threats

(B.) Demands

(C.) Requests

Page 66 Answers

Fill in the Blank

Every relationship has <u>weaknesses</u> and areas of <u>growth</u>.

Page 67 Answers

Multiple Choice: Choose all that apply

"My partner should just love me for who I am and never bring up any issues about me or the relationship" is a:

    A. Healthy perspective

    B. Reasonable viewpoint and totally attainable

    (C.) Belief that comes from an unhealed inner child

    (D.) Fantasy

Fill in the Blank

Instead of viewing yourself as good or bad, great or terrible, begin viewing yourself as <u>great</u> in some areas and in need of <u>growth</u> in other areas.

Put a mark through the toxic beliefs and circle the healthy beliefs:

A. ~~I'm either a good partner or a bad one. Period.~~

B. ~~I either meet all of my partner's needs, or I meet none of them.~~

(C.) I bring a lot to this relationship, and I also have areas of growth I need to address.

D. ~~If my partner doesn't gush over every single part of me, it means they think I'm terrible.~~

(E.) My partner likes many things about me, and there are also areas they'd like me to improve.

F. ~~My partner bringing up an issue about me or the relationship means they don't like me and I'm not good enough.~~

(G.) My partner bringing up an issue about me or the relationship means they care so much about the relationship that they want to put energy into growing and healing it.

Fill in the Blank

All relationships <u>evolve</u>. It's your choice whether your relationship <u>evolves</u> in a conscious, proactive way, or in an unconscious way.

Fill in the Blank

Refusing to examine your contributing factors in relationship issues means you are seeking a parent-child dynamic, and within that dynamic, you are the child. (Psychologically and emotionally speaking, that is.)

Page 75 Answers

Fill in the Blank

<u>Everybody</u> struggles with communication, so don't beat yourself up.

Multiple Choice: Choose all that apply

Unhealthy communication looks like:

(A.) Deflecting issues

B. Speaking directly yet respectfully

(C.) Avoiding issues

(D.) Blaming

E. Getting curious about the situation

(F.) Not examining your role in the situation

Healthy communication looks like:

(A.) Actively working through issues

B. Only describing how the other person is doing or saying wrong or hurtful things

(C.) Squarely facing difficult issues and conversations

D. Evading conversations and hoping the issues will just go away

(E.) Speaking respectfully without sacrificing what you mean to say

(F.) Utilizing a both/and attitude rather than an either/or attitude

Page 76 Answers

Fill in the Blank

A novice communicator expects a <u>straight-line</u> process when communicating.

A seasoned communicator knows there will be dozens of <u>adjustments</u> along the way.

You'll be happier when you forget how things "<u>should</u>" be and begin addressing situations as they are.

Made in United States
Troutdale, OR
12/21/2024

27032890R00062